Tales—
Princesses, Peas,
and Enchanted Trees

Ron Benson
Lynn Bryan
Kim Newlove
Charolette Player
Liz Stenson

CONSULTANTS

Kathyrn D'Angelo

Susan Elliott-Johns

Diane Lomond

Ken MacInnis

Elizabeth Parchment

Prentice Hall Ginn Canada
Scarborough, Ontario

Contents

Bibliography

🎧   Selections with this symbol are available on audio.

  This symbol indicates student writing.

❦   Canadian selections are marked with this symbol.

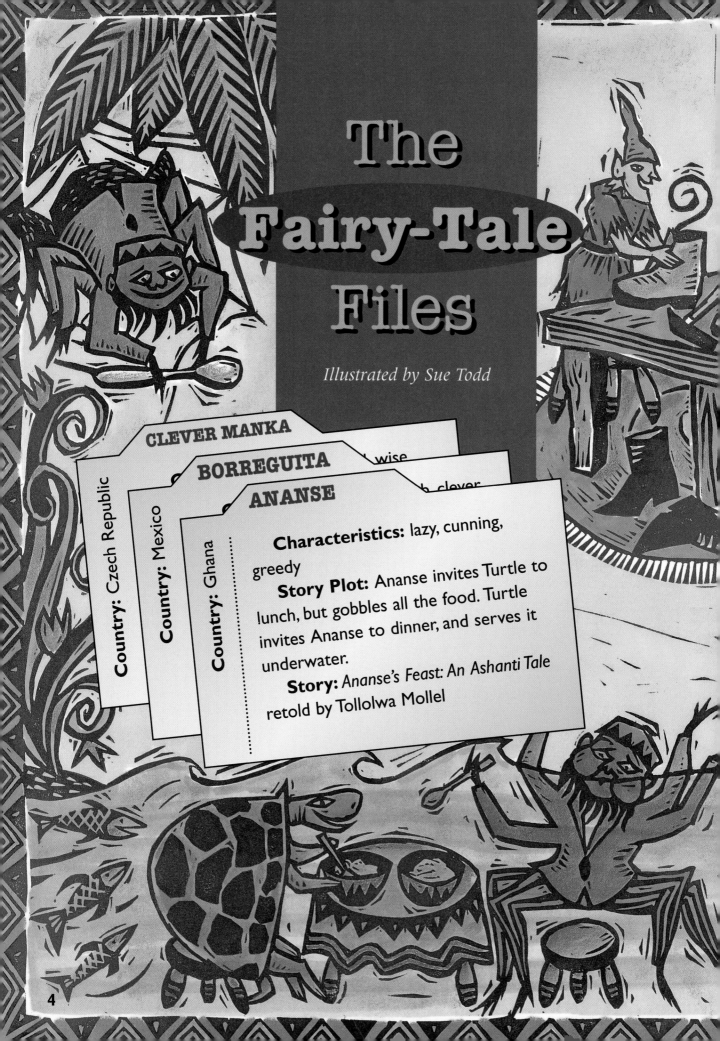

The Fairy-Tale Files

Illustrated by Sue Todd

CLEVER MANKA

Country: Czech Republic

BORREGUITA

Country: Mexico

ANANSE

Country: Ghana

Characteristics: lazy, cunning, greedy

Story Plot: Ananse invites Turtle to lunch, but gobbles all the food. Turtle invites Ananse to dinner, and serves it underwater.

Story: *Ananse's Feast: An Ashanti Tale* retold by Tollolwa Mollel

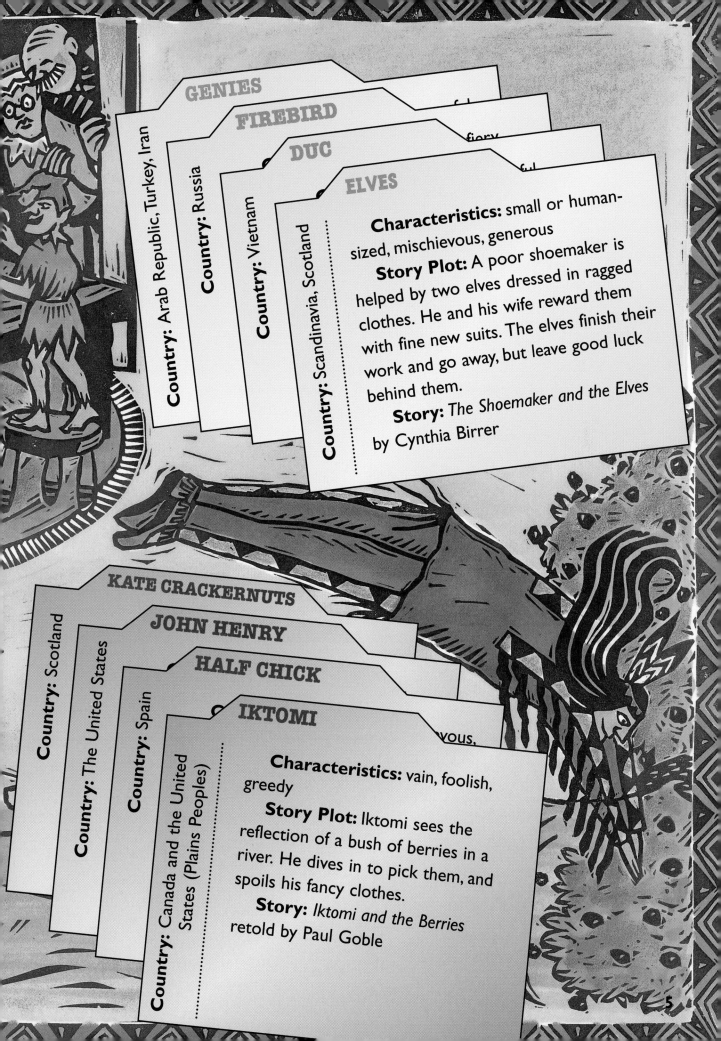

GENIES

Country: Arab Republic, Turkey, Iran

FIREBIRD

Country: Russia

DUC

Country: Vietnam

ELVES

Country: Scandinavia, Scotland

Characteristics: small or human-sized, mischievous, generous

Story Plot: A poor shoemaker is helped by two elves dressed in ragged clothes. He and his wife reward them with fine new suits. The elves finish their work and go away, but leave good luck behind them.

Story: *The Shoemaker and the Elves* by Cynthia Birrer

KATE CRACKERNUTS

Country: Scotland

JOHN HENRY

Country: The United States

HALF CHICK

Country: Spain

IKTOMI

Country: Canada and the United States (Plains Peoples)

Characteristics: vain, foolish, greedy

Story Plot: Iktomi sees the reflection of a bush of berries in a river. He dives in to pick them, and spoils his fancy clothes.

Story: *Iktomi and the Berries* retold by Paul Goble

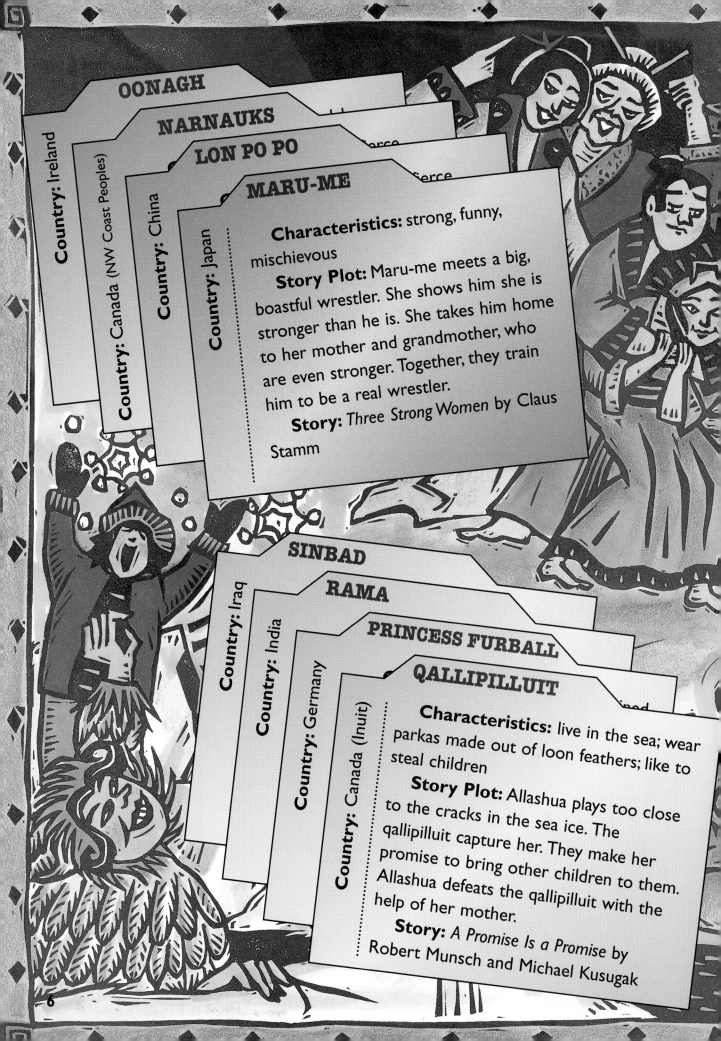

OONAGH

Country: Ireland

NARNAUKS

Country: Canada (NW Coast Peoples)

LON PO PO

Country: China

MARU-ME

Country: Japan

Characteristics: strong, funny, mischievous

Story Plot: Maru-me meets a big, boastful wrestler. She shows him she is stronger than he is. She takes him home to her mother and grandmother, who are even stronger. Together, they train him to be a real wrestler.

Story: *Three Strong Women* by Claus Stamm

SINBAD

Country: Iraq

RAMA

Country: India

PRINCESS FURBALL

Country: Germany

QALLIPILLUIT

Country: Canada (Inuit)

Characteristics: live in the sea; wear parkas made out of loon feathers; like to steal children

Story Plot: Allashua plays too close to the cracks in the sea ice. The qallipilluit capture her. They make her promise to bring other children to them. Allashua defeats the qallipilluit with the help of her mother.

Story: *A Promise Is a Promise* by Robert Munsch and Michael Kusugak

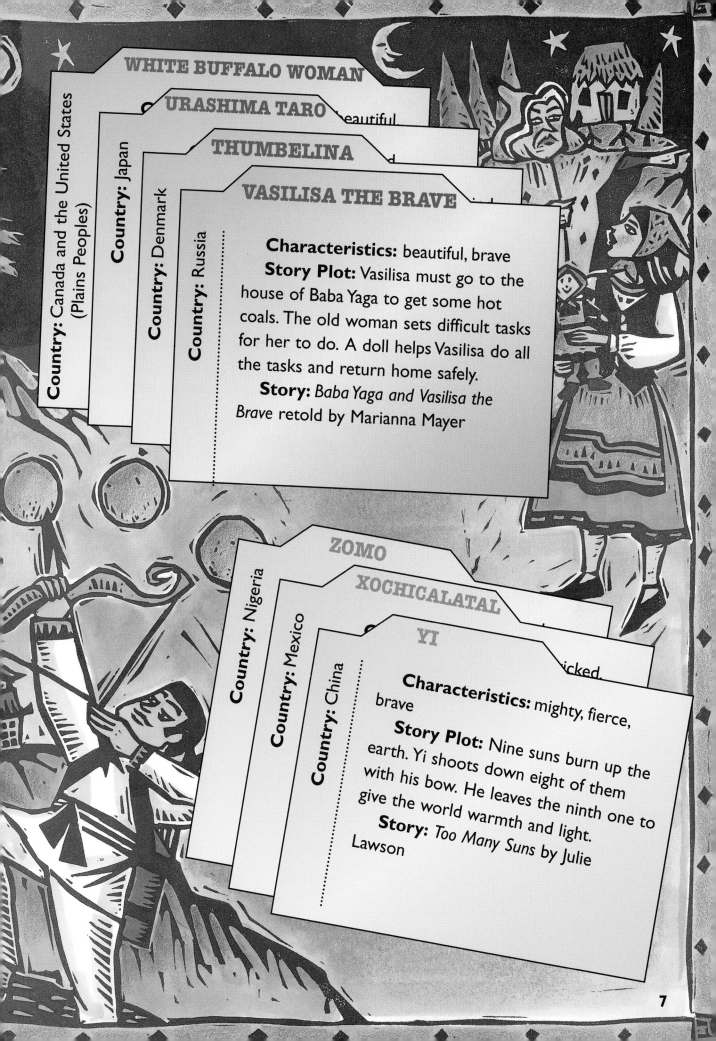

WHITE BUFFALO WOMAN

Country: Canada and the United States (Plains Peoples)

URASHIMA TARO

Country: Japan

THUMBELINA

Country: Denmark

VASILISA THE BRAVE

Country: Russia

Characteristics: beautiful, brave

Story Plot: Vasilisa must go to the house of Baba Yaga to get some hot coals. The old woman sets difficult tasks for her to do. A doll helps Vasilisa do all the tasks and return home safely.

Story: *Baba Yaga and Vasilisa the Brave* retold by Marianna Mayer

ZOMO

Country: Nigeria

XOCHICALATAL

Country: Mexico

YI

Country: China

Characteristics: mighty, fierce, brave

Story Plot: Nine suns burn up the earth. Yi shoots down eight of them with his bow. He leaves the ninth one to give the world warmth and light.

Story: *Too Many Suns* by Julie Lawson

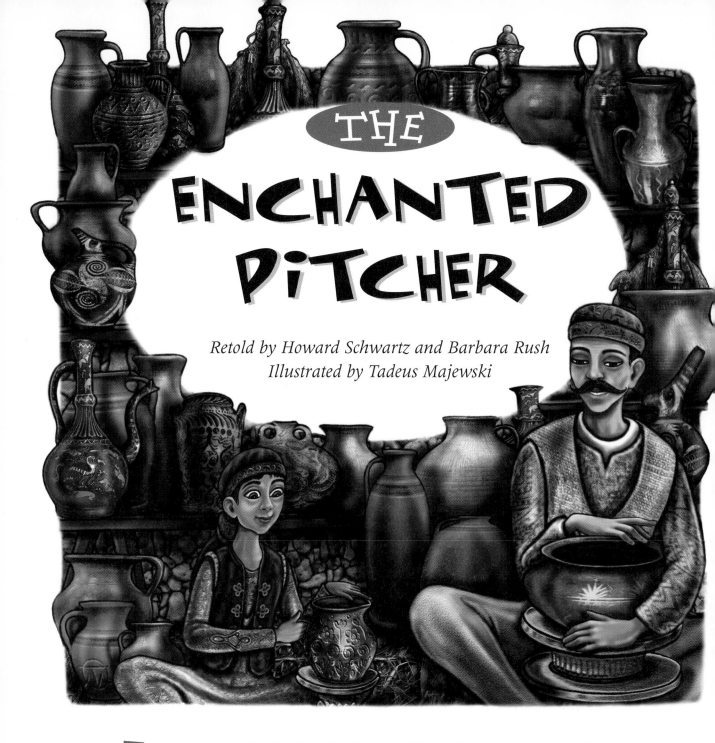

THE ENCHANTED PITCHER

Retold by Howard Schwartz and Barbara Rush
Illustrated by Tadeus Majewski

Long ago, in the land of Iraq, there lived a potter who was very poor. He worked hard from morning till night, making pots and pitchers, but even so, he barely earned enough to feed his family. This potter had a young daughter whose name was Rachel. She loved to watch her father work.

One day the potter let her make a pot by herself, and she shaped it like a vase. Next she added a handle to make the vase into a pitcher.

Oh, what a beautiful pitcher it was—small and round and perfectly formed. Rachel painted lovely flowers on it and decorated the handle with olive leaves. Then she held it in her hands and looked inside. To her surprise, she saw a little puddle of olive oil at the bottom! And as she watched, the oil rose slowly in the pitcher.

"Father, Father," she called. "Come see!"

Her father came running. "It's a miracle," he cried. He sniffed the precious oil and watched it rise, as if it was enchanted.

The pitcher filled itself with oil to the very rim—and then stopped. Rachel and her father dipped their fingers into the oil and tasted it. Much to their delight, they discovered that it was the finest oil they had ever tasted.

"How I wish we could give this oil to your grandmother," the potter said. "She hasn't had any olive oil for many months."

"Oh, Father, let me take it to her," Rachel said.

Her father answered, "No, Rachel, it is too far to Grandmother's house, and you are too young to go by yourself." But Rachel begged and pleaded and promised she would be careful, and at last her father agreed to let her go.

The potter hitched their only donkey to a wooden cart. He carefully loaded the pitcher filled with olive oil. Then he added four jugs that were closed with corks. Rachel was to take these to Grandmother, too. One jug was filled with milk, another with honey, one with wine, and one with vinegar. Finally Rachel kissed her father goodbye and set out on the long road to Grandmother's house.

Rachel drove the cart very slowly so the pitcher would not be shaken. But soon the cart went over a little bump in the road, and some of the olive oil spilled out.

Oh, dear, Rachel thought, how will I ever get this oil to Grandmother's house without spilling it?

Just then she heard a scratchy voice from somewhere inside the wagon. "Rachel, the road to your grandmother's house is very long. I can get you there in a wink, but you must give me all of your oil."

Now, Rachel was not the least bit frightened when she heard that voice. In fact, she was angry—and even though she didn't know who she was speaking to, she said, "What good would it do if I arrived without the oil? No, thank you. I will get to Grandmother's by myself."

There was no answer. Rachel drove on. But she had gone only a little farther down the road when she passed over another bump, and a little more of the oil spilled out.

As Rachel was wondering what to do, the scratchy voice piped up again, "Rachel, I can get you to Grandmother's in a wink, but you must give me all of your oil."

Again Rachel said, "No, thank you, I will get there by myself." And on she drove.

She had gone only a little farther down the road when the cart struck a huge bump and almost tipped over. Nearly all the oil spilled out. Rachel felt like crying. What should she do now? Again the voice spoke up, "Rachel, I can get you to Grandmother's in a wink, but you must give me all of your oil."

By this time Rachel knew that the voice was coming from one of the jugs. She became furious. "Where are you, you naughty thing? It was *you* who caused the oil to spill!" She began to pull the corks out of the jugs. There was nothing odd in the jug of milk, nor in the jug of honey, nor in the jug of wine. But when she pulled the cork out of the vinegar jug, *poof!* Rachel suddenly found herself sitting in front of her grandmother's house.

"H-h-how did I get here?" Rachel asked aloud. And from behind her a scratchy voice answered, "Rachel, it was I who brought you here."

Rachel quickly turned around. A little man was sitting on the floor of the cart. His pants and shirt were baggy, and he wore a stocking cap on his head. He looked very annoyed indeed.

"I am the imp who was hiding in the jug of vinegar," he said. "You pulled out the cork, so I brought you here as quick as a wink. You never promised me the oil, but that oil should be *mine!*" he cried. He stamped his foot in anger. Then he vanished into thin air.

Rachel was relieved that the imp was gone. She jumped down from the cart and hurried to the door.

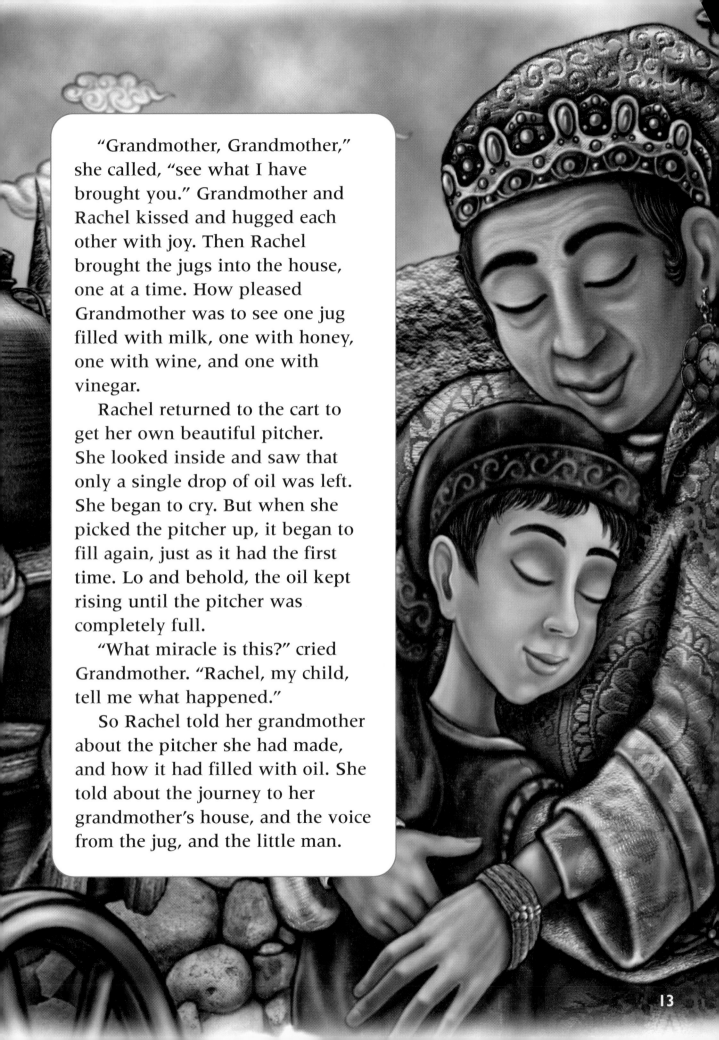

"Grandmother, Grandmother," she called, "see what I have brought you." Grandmother and Rachel kissed and hugged each other with joy. Then Rachel brought the jugs into the house, one at a time. How pleased Grandmother was to see one jug filled with milk, one with honey, one with wine, and one with vinegar.

Rachel returned to the cart to get her own beautiful pitcher. She looked inside and saw that only a single drop of oil was left. She began to cry. But when she picked the pitcher up, it began to fill again, just as it had the first time. Lo and behold, the oil kept rising until the pitcher was completely full.

"What miracle is this?" cried Grandmother. "Rachel, my child, tell me what happened."

So Rachel told her grandmother about the pitcher she had made, and how it had filled with oil. She told about the journey to her grandmother's house, and the voice from the jug, and the little man.

Her grandmother nodded wisely. "Rachel," she said, "you have made an enchanted pitcher. If you had taken the imp's offer, the pitcher would never have filled with oil again. Now it will always fill again, whenever you hold it in your hands."

And that is exactly what happened. Rachel poured that wonderful olive oil into every empty jug in her grandmother's house. Together they put the jugs into the cart and took them to the village to sell. This time Rachel's cart did not hit a single bump, nor did she spill a single drop of oil. Soon there were enough gold coins to buy Grandmother everything she would need for a long, long time.

From then on, the enchanted pitcher supplied all the olive oil Rachel could ever use. Whenever she wished for more, she simply held the pitcher in her hands.

And so it was that Rachel and her family were never poor again—and they gladly shared the wealth from their enchanted pitcher with all those who were in need.

The Princess and the Pea

by Hans Christian Andersen
Illustrated by Tomie dePaola

Once upon a time there was a Prince and he wanted a Princess; but she would have to be a *real* princess. He travelled all around the world to find one, but always there was something wrong. There were Princesses enough, but he found it difficult to make out whether they were *real* ones. There was always something about them that was not quite right. So he came home again and was very sad, for he would have liked very much to have a real Princess.

One evening a terrible storm came on; it thundered and lightened, and the rain poured down in torrents. It was really dreadful! Suddenly a knocking was heard at the city gate, and the old King himself went to open it.

It was a Princess standing out there before the gate. But good gracious! What a sight she was after all the rain and the dreadful weather! The water ran down from her hair and her clothes; it ran down into the toes of her shoes and out again at the heels. And yet she said that she was a real Princess.

Yes, we'll soon find that out, thought the old Queen. But she said nothing, went into the bedroom, took all the bedding off the bedstead, and laid a pea at the bottom; then she took twenty mattresses and laid them on the pea, and then twenty eiderdown beds on top of the mattresses.

On this the Princess was to lie all night. In the morning she was asked how she had slept.

"Oh, terribly badly!" said the Princess. "I have scarcely shut my eyes the whole night. Heaven only knows what was in the bed, but I was lying on something hard, so that I am black and blue all over my body. It is really terrible."

Now they knew that she was a real Princess, because she had felt the pea right through the twenty mattresses and the twenty eiderdown beds.

Nobody but a real Princess could be as sensitive as that.

So the Prince took her for his wife, for now he knew that he had a real Princess; and the pea was put in the Art Museum, where it may still be seen, if no one has stolen it.

There, that is the *real* story!

ABOUT THE ILLUSTRATOR TOMIE DePAOLA

By the time Tomie dePaola was four years old, he knew that he would be an artist. Now he has illustrated nearly two hundred books, and has written stories for many of these. His books are in print in more than fifteen countries. Tomie has received many awards for his books, and two libraries have even named their children's rooms after him!

Mr. Frog Went A-Courtin'

by Elaine E. Runyon
Photographed by Gilbert Duclos

Characters

MR. FROG

MS. MOUSE

UNCLE RAT

MOTH

BUG

RACOON

SNAKE

BUMBLEBEE

FLEA

TWO ANTS

FLY

CHICK

HARE

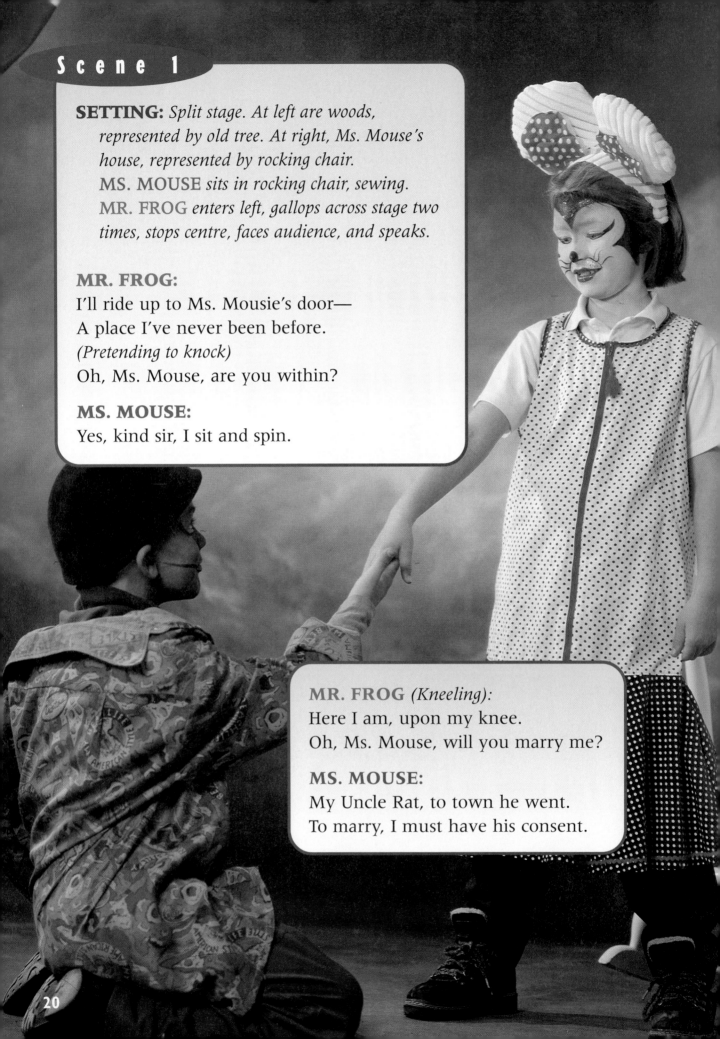

Scene 1

SETTING: *Split stage. At left are woods, represented by old tree. At right, Ms. Mouse's house, represented by rocking chair.*
MS. MOUSE sits in rocking chair, sewing.
MR. FROG enters left, gallops across stage two times, stops centre, faces audience, and speaks.

MR. FROG:
I'll ride up to Ms. Mousie's door—
A place I've never been before.
(Pretending to knock)
Oh, Ms. Mouse, are you within?

MS. MOUSE:
Yes, kind sir, I sit and spin.

MR. FROG *(Kneeling):*
Here I am, upon my knee.
Oh, Ms. Mouse, will you marry me?

MS. MOUSE:
My Uncle Rat, to town he went.
To marry, I must have his consent.

UNCLE RAT *(Entering left):*
Here I am, at last at home.
Who's been here while I was gone?

MS. MOUSE:
Mr. Frog, down on his knee,
Says he wants to marry me.

UNCLE RAT:
Where will the wedding supper be?

MS. MOUSE *and* **MR. FROG**
(Together):
Way down yonder, 'neath the
hollow tree. *(They point left.)*

UNCLE RAT:
Who will make the wedding gown?

MS. MOUSE:
Old Ms. Hare of Berrytown.

UNCLE RAT:
This sounds fine, let's set a date.
Just get ready, and don't be late!
(Curtain)

Scene 2

SETTING: *Meadow, near hollow tree.* **MOTH** *enters, carrying tablecloth.* **NOTE:** *Other characters carry in props as indicated and sit down after they speak their lines.*

MOTH:
I'm the first to come, and I'm Ms. Moth.
I have brought the tablecloth.

BUG *(Entering):*
Here I come, I'm Mr. Bug.
I have brought the cider jug.

MOTH:
What will the wedding supper be?

BUG:
Three green beans and a black-eyed pea.

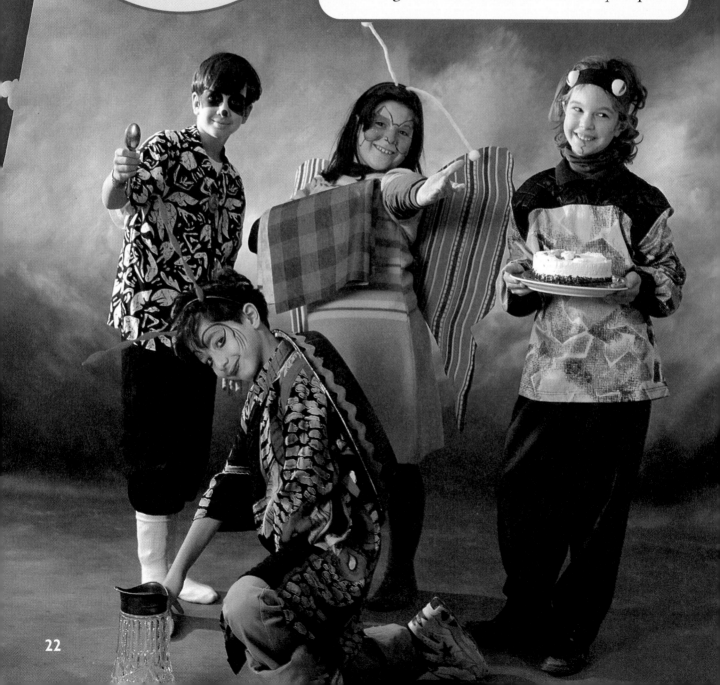

RACOON *(Entering):*
Look at me, I'm Mr. Racoon.
I have brought a silver spoon.
(Remains standing to announce other visitors)

SNAKE *(Entering):*
I'm so pretty, a spotted snake,
I'll pass 'round the wedding cake.

RACOON *(Using spoon as microphone):*
Next to come is the bumblebee.

BUMBLEBEE *(Limping in):*
I have a sore upon my knee.

RACOON:
Next to come is a nimble flea.

FLEA *(Entering):*
I'll dance a jig with the bumblebee.
(Grabs BUMBLEBEE's arm and dances around)

UNCLE RAT *(Entering, crossing centre):*
I'll escort Ms. Mouse, the bride,
Right down to Mr. Froggie's side.

RACOON:
Next to come, two little ants.

ANTS *(Entering):*
We came here to dance and dance.

RACOON:
A fly (FLY *enters*), a chick (CHICK *enters*), and now a hare (HARE *enters*)—
All the guests are gathered there.
(MR. FROG enters left, stands by tree. UNCLE RAT meets MS. MOUSE, carrying flowers, right, escorts her to MR. FROG.)

MR. FROG *(To all guests):*
We'll all sit down and eat some pie.

MS. MOUSE:
Gather 'round and don't be shy.

FLY:
What's the matter with Mr. Chick?

CHICK *(Bent over, holding stomach):*
I ate so much it made me sick.

MS. MOUSE:
Now I'm ready to throw the flowers.
(Does so)

MOTH *(Catching flowers):*
Come, let's dance for hours and hours!
*(All dance, joining hands with partners
and skipping around.)*

RACOON *(Announcing to audience):*
Frog and Mouse went to France,
And that's the end of this romance.
*(All sing "Mr. Frog Went A-Courtin'."
Curtain)*

The Name of the Tree

by Celia Barker Lottridge
Illustrated by Ian Wallace

O nce, long ago, in the land of the short grass, there was a great hunger. No rain fell, and no grass grew.

The ostrich, the gazelle, the giraffe, the monkey, the rabbit, the tortoise, the zebra, and all the other animals were hungry. They searched in the jungle, they searched by the river, they searched on the great flat plain, but they could find nothing to eat.

At last all the animals gathered together and they said, "Let us go together across the great flat plain until we come to something we can eat."

And so all the animals, except for the lion, who was king and lived in the jungle, walked across the flat, empty land. They walked and walked. After many days, they saw a small bump on the edge of the flat land.

Then they saw that the small bump was a tree.

And the tree was very tall.

And the tree had fruit on it, such fruit as they had never seen before.

It was as red as pomegranates, as yellow as bananas, as green as melons, as purple as plums, as orange as mangoes, and it smelled like all the fruits of the world.

But the tree was so tall and the branches so high that even the giraffe couldn't reach the fruit. And the trunk was so smooth that even the monkey couldn't climb the tree.

The animals sat on the ground and cried because the fruit smelled so good and they were so hungry.

At last, when they were too tired to cry any longer, a very old tortoise spoke.

"O animals," she said, "my great-great-great-grandmother told me a story about a wonderful tree. The fruit of that tree was delicious and good to eat. But it could be reached only by those who knew the name of the tree."

The animals cried out, "But who can tell us the name of the tree?"

The very old tortoise answered, "The king knows. We must send someone to ask him."

"I will go," said the gazelle. "I am the fastest runner of us all." And that was true.

So the gazelle started out across the great flat plain. He ran like an arrow shot from a bow, and as he ran he thought, How lucky the animals are that I am willing to go to the king. No one can run as fast as I.

Indeed, it was not long before the gazelle reached the jungle and the place by the river where the king lived.

The king was sitting with his tail neatly wrapped around him. Every hair in his golden coat lay smooth and shining. He spoke kindly to the gazelle. "What do you wish of me," he said.

"O great king," said the gazelle, "all the animals are hungry and we have found a tree filled with wonderful fruit. But we cannot eat the fruit until we know the name of the tree."

"I will tell you," said the lion, "but you must remember, for I don't want to have to tell anyone else. The name of the tree is Ungalli."

"Ungalli," said the gazelle. "I will run as fast as the wind and I will reach the tree before I can possibly forget."

The gazelle thanked the king and began to run through the jungle and across the great flat plain. He thought about how happy all the animals would be, and how they would thank him and be grateful to him. He thought about this so hard that he did not see a rabbit hole that lay in his path, not far from where the animals were waiting. He stepped in it and went head over hoofs over head over hoofs. He landed in a heap at the foot of the tree.

"What is the name of the tree?" shouted the animals.

The gazelle shook his head. He shook it again. But the name was gone. "I can't remember," he whispered.

The animals groaned. "We will have to send someone else," they said. "Someone who will not forget."

"I will go," said the elephant. "I never forget anything."

The animals nodded, for this was true. And so the elephant strode off across the great flat plain.

"I will not forget," she said to herself. "I can remember anything

I choose to. Even the names of all my cousins." The elephant had hundreds of cousins. "Or the names of all the stars in the sky."

When the elephant arrived at the edge of the river, the king was sitting in his usual place, but the end of his tail was twitching and his fur was ruffled.

"What do you want," he growled.

"O king," said the elephant, "all the animals are hungry . . ."

"I know," said the lion, "and you want to know the name of the tree with the wonderful fruit. I will tell you, but don't you forget because I absolutely will not tell anyone else. The name of the tree is Ungalli."

"I will not forget," said the elephant haughtily. "I never forget anything." And she turned and began to make her way out of the jungle.

"Forget," she grumbled to herself. "Me, forget! Why, I can remember the names of all the trees in this jungle." And she began to name them. When she had finished the jungle trees, she went on to all the other trees in Africa. She was just starting on the trees of the rest of the world when she happened to step in the very rabbit hole that had tripped the gazelle. Her foot fitted exactly into the hole, so exactly that she couldn't get it out.

The animals waiting under the tree saw the elephant and ran toward her calling, "What is the name of the tree?"

The elephant pulled and tugged and pulled and tugged, and at last with a great *pop* her foot came out of the hole.

"I can't remember," she said crossly, "and I don't care. That tree has caused far too much trouble already."

The animals didn't even groan. They were too tired and too hungry.

After a long time a very young tortoise spoke.

"O animals," he said, "I will go and find out the name of the tree."

"You!" said the animals. "But you are so young and you are so small and you are so slow."

"Yes," said the very young tortoise. "But I know how to remember. I learned from my great-great-great-grandmother, the one who told you about the tree."

The animals had nothing to say. And the little tortoise was already on his way. It is true that he was slow. But by putting one short leg ahead of the other he crossed the great flat plain, went through the jungle, and arrived at the place by the river where the king lived.

The king was not sitting in his usual place. He was pacing up and down the bank of the river, waving his tail. His fur was standing on end.

When he saw the very young tortoise, he roared, "If you have come to ask me the name of the tree, go home. I have told the gazelle and I have told the elephant that the name of the tree is Ungalli, and I will *not* tell you."

The very young tortoise nodded his head politely. He turned and began to walk out of the jungle.

As he walked he said, "Ungalli, Ungalli, the name of the tree is Ungalli. Ungalli, Ungalli, the name of the tree is Ungalli."

And he went on saying it as he crossed the great flat plain. "Ungalli, Ungalli, the name of the tree is Ungalli."

And he never stopped saying it, even when he got tired, even when he got thirsty. Because that is what his great-great-great-grandmother had told him to do. Even when he fell right to the bottom of that same rabbit hole, the very young tortoise just climbed out saying, "Ungalli, Ungalli, the name of the tree is Ungalli."

None of the animals saw him coming. They were sitting under the tree, looking at the ground. The very young tortoise walked straight up to the foot of the tree and said in a loud voice, "The name of the tree is Ungalli!"

The animals looked up.

They saw the branches of the tree bend down so low that they could reach the wonderful fruit that was as red as pomegranates, as yellow as bananas, as green as melons, as purple as plums, and as orange as mangoes, and smelled like all the fruits of the world.

The animals ate. They ate until they could eat no more. And then they lifted the very young tortoise high in the air and marched around the tree chanting, "Ungalli, Ungalli, the name of the tree is Ungalli," because they did not want to forget. And they never did.

ABOUT THE AUTHOR CELIA BARKER LOTTRIDGE

Celia Barker Lottridge helped found the Storytellers School of Toronto. She performs and runs workshops on storytelling for both children and adults. Celia has also written several picture books for children, and three novels.

Characters and Ideas Used in Fairy Tales

Most fairy tales have magic. They all have about five characters. Most of the stories have princes and a king. Lots of fairy tales take place in castles. They usually start with "once upon a time." Lots have three little pigs or wolves and snakes.

Morgan Empey
Grade 3

I like knowing what's happening in other parts of the world.

Morgan Empey

The Princess and the Frog

Once upon a time there was a king who had five daughters. The oldest one had a purple shiny ball that was her favorite toy. One day she went to the pond with her sisters. When they got there, they played with the purple shiny ball until it fell into the pond. The oldest princess asked her sisters to try to get her the ball, but they couldn't reach it. Suddenly the princess heard the voice of a frog. He said, "If you give me something of yours I will get you your ball." The frog dove in and got the ball. The frog said, "Will you let me sleep in your bed and drink from your golden cup and eat from your golden plate?" "I promise," said the princess. The next day the frog burst into the room where the princess sat with her father. He ate all of her food and drank all of her drink! Then he went to sleep in her bed. Suddenly something weird happened. The frog turned into a prince! After that, they got married, and the purple shiny ball was kept in a glass case on an orange pillow!! The end.

Kelsi Newlove
Grade 3

I like to write because it's fun and it makes me think about stuff.

Kelsi Newlove

Cinderella
Around the World

by Sharon Stewart
Photographed by Peter Chou

A glass slipper, a fairy godmother, and a coach that turns into a pumpkin. Do these things remind you of anything? Of course they do—the fairy tale "Cinderella."

What Is a Cinderella Story?

The Cinderella story many people know was written long ago by a French writer named Charles Perrault. He called his story "Little Cinder, or the Little Glass Slipper."

Here is how the Cinderella story goes. A good, kind girl is treated badly by her cruel stepmother and stepsisters. Because she huddles in the ashes, or cinders, of the fireplace to keep warm, they call her Cinderella.

One day a great ball is held at the palace. Cinderella's fairy godmother appears and gives her a beautiful gown and a pair of dainty glass slippers. Then the godmother turns a pumpkin into a coach and six white mice into white horses to pull it. She warns Cinderella that the enchantment will only last until midnight.

Cinderella goes to the ball for three nights and dances with the prince. On the third night, she forgets the time. The clock strikes twelve, and she rushes from the palace. In her hurry, she loses one of her glass slippers.

The prince searches for the girl whose foot fits the slipper. At last, he finds Cinderella. The slipper fits, and she pulls the matching one out of her pocket. Cinderella and the prince live happily ever after.

A World of Cinderellas

Stories very much like this Cinderella tale are told all around the world. Some parts of the stories may be different, but some things are the same in many of them. For example, the good, kind hero always has to work very hard, and she is covered with ashes or dirt. She always receives magical help, though not always from a fairy godmother. Often, there is an object, like a slipper, that helps a prince or king find her, and her goodness is rewarded in the end.

Here are some other Cinderella stories from around the world.

China

The world's oldest Cinderella story comes from China. Yeh-shen, the Chinese Cinderella, is also mistreated by a cruel stepmother. Her magic helper is a fish, and she goes to a festival in a cloak woven of blue and gold feathers, wearing slippers of gold. On the way home, Yeh-shen drops one of her golden slippers. Someone finds it and sells it to the king. Then he searches his kingdom for its owner. At last he finds Yeh-shen and makes her his wife.

Nigeria

In a tale from Nigeria, the magic helper is a frog. A kind maiden feeds frogs in a pond near her house. When the chief gives a dance festival, the frogs give her fine clothes and a pair of slippers, one of silver and one of gold. The maiden loses the golden slipper when she runs away from the dance. At last the chief's son finds her, and the golden slipper hops right onto her foot.

Ireland

Have you ever heard of a *boy* Cinderella? In an Irish tale, Billy Beg, the son of a king, has many adventures. Then he rescues a princess from a terrible sea dragon. As he rides away, the princess

catches hold of his very large boot, which he leaves behind him. Of course she finds the lad who fits the boot, and they live happily ever after.

Algonquin Peoples: Canada and the United States

The Cinderella of the Algonquin Peoples of Canada and the United States is called the Rough-Face Girl. She lives in a village with her sisters, who treat her cruelly. In the same village lives an invisible being. His sister says he will only marry the maiden who can truly see him. The sisters of Rough-Face Girl try in vain to describe him. Then Rough-Face Girl tries. Everyone laughs at her, yet she succeeds. She sees a noble warrior whose bow is the rainbow and whose sled runners are the Milky Way. They marry and live happily ever after.

Japan

Benizara, the Japanese Cinderella, wins her prince by cleverness instead of a magic slipper. She too is badly treated by her stepmother and stepsister. One day an old woman gives her a little box. She tells Benizara it will give her what she wants. Soon a play is performed in the village. Benizara pulls a beautiful kimono out of the box, and goes happily to the play. A nobleman sees her there, and the next day he visits her house. He puts a pile of salt on a plate, and sticks a single pine needle in it. Then he challenges Benizara and her stepsister to make up poems about it. The stepsister makes up an ugly poem about a pile of salt, but Benizara's poem describes a snowy mountain with a lonely pine tree.

The nobleman is so delighted with her cleverness that he marries her at once.

Some people think there are as many as seven hundred Cinderella tales. Did just one story spread around the world? Or did many stories spring up in many lands? No one knows for sure. One thing is certain, though. People everywhere still tell Cinderella tales, and even write new ones. Of course, none of them is true—is it? Just in case, though, you might want to look out for fairy godmothers, and be very kind to frogs and fish. Above all, watch what you do with your shoes!

The Hare and the Tortoise

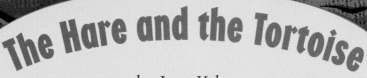

by Jane Yolen
Illustrated by Sylvie Bourbonnière

"Slowpoke, lowpoke,"
Called the hare.
"You no-go-poke
Anywhere."

Tortoise answered,
"Slow as day,
I'll outrun you
Anyway."

An oval racetrack
They laid out
To prove the faster
Without doubt.

Out in front
Hare quickly leapt,
While steady, steady
Tortoise crept.

Then halfway there,
Hare took a nap,
So tortoise caught him
On that lap.

Hare dreamed his winning
Quite away,
And tortoise took
The prize that day.

Moral:
If naps and laps
You do confuse,
Then you are surely
Bound to lose.

FINISH

The Extraordinary Cat

Retold by Pleasant DeSpain
Illustrated by Hélène Bouliane

Once there was a Chinese ruler who had a cat that he treasured above all other animals. He loved the cat so much and thought that it was so extraordinary that he named it Sky.

One day soon after, an advisor to the court spoke to the ruler and explained, "There is something much more powerful than the sky, and that is the cloud. The cloud can darken and even hide the sky from view."

"Quite right," agreed the ruler. "From this day forth, my beautiful cat shall be called Cloud."

Two weeks later the ruler's wife said, "Dear husband, I don't think that Cloud is a proper name for your cat. There is something stronger than the cloud, and that is the wind that blows the cloud about."

"Indeed! From now on my superior cat will be called Wind. Here Wind! Here Wind! Nice little Wind."

During the next month, the ruler's brother came for a visit and agreed that the cat was the most extraordinary animal he had ever seen. "But," he said, "Wind is not a suitable name for this superb creature. The wind is servant to that which it cannot penetrate . . . such as a wall. The wall is stronger than the wind."

"I hadn't thought of that," replied the ruler, "and you are to be congratulated, brother, for being so observant. From now on, my dearest cat, the most wonderful cat on earth, will be called Wall."

The very next day the royal gardener heard the ruler call his cat "Wall," and said, "But sire, you are forgetting that a mouse is able to chew a hole in a wall. The mouse is the strongest."

"How clever of you," said the ruler. "From this day forth, my lovely cat will be called Mouse. Come here, Mouse!"

But just then the ruler's boy and girl skipped into the garden to play, and when they heard their father call the cat "Mouse," they started to laugh and laugh!

"What causes you to laugh, children?" asked the ruler.

"Father," replied the little girl, "everyone knows that there is something stronger than the mouse, and that's the cat who catches it!"

The ruler smiled as he realized that his children were the wisest of all his advisors. Then he began to laugh. "Of course! How foolish I've been. From now on my extraordinary animal will be called by the name he most deserves, and that is Cat!"

ABOUT THE AUTHOR

PLEASANT DeSPAIN

Pleasant DeSpain has liked writing and telling stories ever since he was in Grade Three. He is now the author of six books, and he has travelled all over the world collecting stories. He tells these stories to children through his television program, his newspaper column, and in person.

Mother Holle

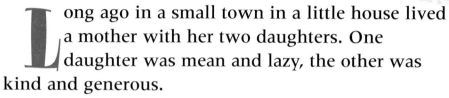

Retold by Charlotte Dorn
Illustrated by France Brassard

Long ago in a small town in a little house lived a mother with her two daughters. One daughter was mean and lazy, the other was kind and generous.

One day while the kind girl was spinning wool for a sweater, her spindle fell down the water well. Her angry mother told her she must find it. The girl was very afraid, but she closed her eyes and jumped down into the well.

When she opened her eyes she found herself in a strange world. Near her stood a huge oven full of bread. The oven began to cry:

"Help me! Help me! Take out my bread or it will burn."

So the girl took all the sweet-smelling loaves of bread out of the oven. When she turned around she saw an apple tree who cried:

"Help me! Help me! Pick my apples or my branches will break."

So the girl picked all the ripe red apples off the tree.

She walked on and came to the house of an old woman who lived up in the clouds with her cat.

The old woman asked the girl to stay with her and do all her work for her.

She said to the girl:

"You must be careful how you shake my pillows. The feathers will have to fly and blow about. Then it will snow on earth. I am Mother Holle."

The children on earth knew all about Mother Holle. They loved her and used to sing to her:

Mother Holle, Mother Holle
shake your pillows
make it snow

Mother Holle, Mother Holle
shake your pillows
we love snow

So the girl stayed with Mother Holle for a long time, and she was happy.

Then one day she became very sad and said to Mother Holle:

"I have been happy with you and will miss you, but I am homesick and need to see my mother and sister again."

Mother Holle replied:

"You have done your work well. You have made the children on earth and me happy. I will give you a gift and the spindle you lost. Then I will show you the way home."

She took the girl to a huge gate, and when the gate opened a shower of golden coins rained upon the girl, covering her so that she looked like a ray of sunshine coming back to earth.

The rooster, the mother, and the lazy sister saw her coming home, and the rooster crowed:

"Cock-a-doodle-do, your golden girl is coming back to you."

Her mother and her sister were truly amazed and took the golden girl into the house where she told them her story.

Now the mother wanted the same kind of luck for her other daughter. So the lazy girl threw the spindle down the water well and jumped in after it.

She found herself in the same strange place as her sister. The oven stood there and cried:

"Help me! Help me! Take out my bread or it will burn."

But the girl replied:

"Oven, I will do no such thing, for you might get me dirty."

The apple tree was there and cried:

"Help me! Help me! Pick my apples or my branches will break."

But the girl replied:

"Apple tree, I will do no such thing, for your apples might fall on my head."

When the lazy girl reached the house of Mother Holle she offered to work for her.

On the first day she did her job well, then she became lazier and lazier until finally she did nothing at all.

45

She did not even shake Mother Holle's feather pillows. So it did not snow on earth anymore and the children were sad.

Mother Holle became angry and said:

"You must go home. I will show you the way."

She took the girl to the same huge gate, but this time when the gate opened, a shower of ashes poured upon the girl, covering her so that she looked like a scarecrow coming back to earth.

The rooster and the mother saw her coming home, and the rooster crowed:

"Cock-a-doodle-do, your dirty girl is coming back to you."

And as long as the lazy girl lived she looked dirty. The ashes never came off no matter how hard she scrubbed and rubbed and washed herself.

ABOUT THE AUTHOR CHARLOTTE DORN

Charlotte Dorn was born in Berlin but she now lives in Kingston, Ontario. She is considered an expert on children's books from around the world. Charlotte translated this Brothers Grimm story from German because "it's a wonderful tale about the winter—and Canada has a lot of that!"

How Eagle Got His Good Eyes

by Grade 5 students at Oscar Blackburn School
Illustrated by Grade 7 students at Oscar Blackburn School

 long, long time ago in northern Canada, there lived Eagle. Eagle had no eyes. He always bumped into trees and crashed into bushes.

He could catch some animals because he could hear and smell well. But Eagle didn't catch much food because he couldn't see.

A man lived near Eagle. His name was Nanabush. Nanabush was a trickster. He would trick any animal if he had the chance.

Nanabush wanted to be chief of all his people. He thought that he needed a headdress.

With a headdress, I could become chief, he thought.

He knew that Eagle had the biggest and the best feathers. Nanabush decided to shoot Eagle to get the feathers.

Nanabush tried and tried to shoot Eagle. But he couldn't shoot the bird because Eagle was flying too fast and too high.

Nanabush had to get a new idea.

Nanabush put a net between two trees. He tied jackfish and pickerel to the net. Then, he hung a giant sturgeon from one of the trees. Eagle would smell that for sure.

Not far away, Eagle was very hungry. He was really surprised and excited when he smelled the fish.

Eagle followed the smell. He crashed into many trees but he did reach the fish . . . and the net.

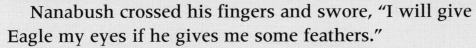

Eagle was very angry and he waved his claws.

Nanabush was afraid to go near Eagle. He had no more arrows, so he decided to make a deal with the bird.

Nanabush said, "I want some feathers. What do you want?"

Eagle replied, "I'll give you some feathers if you give me your eyeballs."

Eagle made Nanabush swear to the Great Spirit, Manitou.

Nanabush crossed his fingers and swore, "I will give Eagle my eyes if he gives me some feathers."

Nanabush broke the promise. He took fish eyes from the dead sturgeon and put them in Eagle's sockets.

"Where is my eyesight?" Eagle squawked.

Nanabush said, "It's nighttime. You can't see in the dark."

Eagle nodded. "Take ten feathers from my body."

Nanabush plucked fifteen feathers and ran away.

Manitou, the Great Spirit, was watching from the sky. He knew Nanabush broke a vow to him. Manitou was very angry. Using lightning, Manitou gave Eagle really good eyesight. Then he burned away the net that was covering the bird.

Eagle spread his wings and thanked Manitou.

Eagle flew away.

He still didn't fly properly because fifteen feathers were missing.

He saw Nanabush running. Eagle glided down and snatched his feathers from Nanabush's quiver.

Then, he picked up Nanabush and dropped him in a river.

Nanabush had to swim to shore. He was wet and cold. He also lost his quiver and all his food in the water.

Eagle felt sorry for Nanabush. With his good eyesight, Eagle spotted a big fish.

He grabbed it and brought it to Nanabush.

They shared the fish and Nanabush apologized.

They were friends the rest of the season . . . until Nanabush tried to trick Eagle again.

The Lad Who Went to the North Wind

Retold by Anne Rockwell
Illustrated by Kim LaFave

Once upon a time there was a widow who had one son, and he went out to the storehouse to fetch some oatmeal for cooking. But as he was coming back to the house, there came the North Wind, puffing and blowing. The North Wind caught up the oatmeal and blew it away. Then the lad went back to the storehouse for more, but no sooner had he come outside than the North Wind came and blew away the oatmeal with just one puff. Worse yet, the Wind did it a third time.

At this the lad got very angry, and as he thought it mean that the North Wind should behave so, he decided he'd go and find the North Wind and ask him to give back the oatmeal.

So off he went, but the way was long, and he walked and he walked, but at last he came to the North Wind's house.

"Good day," said the lad. "Thank you for coming to see us yesterday."

"Good day!" answered the North Wind in a loud, gruff voice. "Thanks for coming to see me. What do you want?"

"Oh," said the lad, "I only wished to ask you to be so kind as to let me have back that oatmeal you took from me, for my mother and I haven't much to live on. If you're to go on snapping up every morsel we have, we'll starve."

"I haven't got your oatmeal," said the North Wind, "but if you are in such need, I'll give you a cloth that will give you all the food you want if you will only say, 'Cloth, cloth, spread yourself and serve up a good dinner!'"

With this the lad was happy. But as the way was so long he couldn't get home in one day, so he stopped overnight at an inn. He went to sit down to supper, and he laid the cloth on a table and said, "Cloth, cloth, spread yourself and serve up a good dinner!"

And the cloth did.

Everyone at the inn thought this was a wonderful thing, but most of all the landlady. So when everyone was fast asleep, she took the lad's cloth and put another in its place. It looked just like the one the lad had got from the North Wind, but it couldn't serve up even a bit of stale bread.

When the lad woke, he took his cloth and went home to his mother.

"Now," said he, "I've been to the North Wind's house, and a good fellow he is. He gave me this cloth, and when I say to it, 'Cloth, cloth, spread yourself and serve up a good dinner!' I can get all the food I want."

"Seeing is believing," said his mother. "I shan't believe it until I see it."

So the lad made haste, and laid the cloth on the table. Then he said, "Cloth, cloth, spread yourself and serve up a good dinner!"

But the cloth served up nothing, not even a bit of stale bread.

"Well," said the lad, "there is nothing to do but to go to the North Wind again." And away he went.

So he walked and he walked, and late in the afternoon he came to where the North Wind lived.

"Good evening," said the lad.

"Good evening," said the North Wind in a loud, gruff voice.

"I want my rights for that oatmeal of ours you took," said the lad. "As for the cloth I got from you, it isn't worth a penny."

"I've got no oatmeal," said the North Wind. "But I'll give you a goat that gives forth golden coins whenever you say to it, 'Goat, goat, make money!'"

So the lad thought this a fine thing, but it was too far to get home that day, so he turned in for the night at the same inn where he had slept before.

When he was settled, he tried out the goat the North Wind had given him and found it all right, but when the landlord saw the goat give forth golden coins, he changed it for an ordinary goat while the lad slept.

Next morning off went the lad. When he got home, he said to his mother, "What a good fellow the North Wind is! Now he has given me a goat that gives forth golden coins whenever I say, 'Goat, goat, make money!' "

"All very true, I daresay," said his mother. "But I shan't believe it until I see the gold coins made."

"Goat, goat, make money!" said the lad, but the goat didn't.

So the lad went back to the North Wind and got very angry, for he said the goat was worth nothing, and he must have his oatmeal back.

"Well," said the North Wind, "I've nothing else to give you except that old stick in the corner, but it's a stick that if you say, 'Stick, stick, lay on!' lays on until you say, 'Stick, stick, now stop!' "

So, as the way was long, the lad turned in for the night at the same inn. By now he had pretty well guessed what had become of the cloth and the goat, so he lay down on the bed and began to snore, pretending to be asleep.

Now the landlord, who was sure the stick must be worth something, found one just like it. When he heard the lad snore, he was going to exchange the two, but just as he was about to take the stick, the lad yelled out, "Stick, stick, lay on!"

So the stick began to beat the landlord, and the landlord jumped over tables, chairs, and benches, and yelled and roared, "Oh, my! Oh, my! Bid the stick be still, and you shall have both your cloth and your goat!"

So the lad said, "Stick, stick, now stop!"

Then he took the cloth, put it in his pocket, and went home with his stick in his hand, leading the goat by a rope, and so he got his rights for the oatmeal he had lost, and if he didn't live happily ever after, that's not the fault of either you or me.

ABOUT THE AUTHOR ANNE ROCKWELL

Anne Rockwell has written and illustrated many classic children's books. She has published more than eighty books of her own, and nearly thirty books with her husband, Harlow Rockwell. She has also illustrated many books by other authors. She currently lives in Greenwich, Connecticut.

How Hyenas Learned to Laugh

Ryan Cupid

Once in Africa, the hyenas weren't very joyful. They just grumbled and mumbled all the time. Then a monkey threw a banana peel. The wart hog slipped on the peel and the hyenas laughed. From then on all hyenas always laugh.

Ryan Cupid
Grade 3

How the Moon Got Its Light

Four firefly friends were fluttering from their classmate's house on their way to their homes. They were very tired from flying all that way. They stopped and landed on two lily pads to take a rest. A giant frog saw two of the fireflies and, SNAP, one lick of its long tongue and they were gone! The other two fireflies did not know their two friends had been eaten because they were getting a drink of water. They looked everywhere on this planet for their friends! They went to the moon, thinking they were there. They thought the moon was so warm and such a good place to live that they decided to get married and have lots of children. Now, in the night, you can see the moon shining from the glow of their tails.

Dylan Branton
Grade 4

I have two brothers. I decided to write this story because one of my brothers always wondered how the moon got its light.

Dylan Branton

The Finding Princess

by Sue Ann Alderson
Illustrated by Doris Barrette

O nce there was a sad princess. Her mother and father, her grandmother and grandfather, were all sad too, because their princess was sad.

"Tell us what to do to make you happy," said the grown-ups, "and we will do what we can."

So the princess said,

> "Bring me a cup of pearl,
> And a silver ring.
> Give me dancing shoes
> And a bird that sings."

"We will try," said the mother and father, the grandmother and grandfather.

The mother brought a cup of pearl made by twelve jewellers, but it was not quite the right cup.

The father brought a silver ring made by twenty-four silversmiths, but it was not just the right ring.

The grandmother brought dancing shoes embroidered by forty-eight ladies-in-waiting, but they were not at all the right shoes.

The grandfather brought a singing bird adorned and finely made by ninety-six craftsmen, but that was all wrong too.

"We have tried, we have done what we could, but we cannot make you happy," said the grown-ups. "You will have to do that for yourself."

So the princess put on her hiking boots and packed some peanut butter and macaroni sandwiches, some licorice, pickles, and chocolate-chip cookies in a basket, and set out to find for herself what she required.

She walked and she wandered for a long while. She arrived at the seashore where she saw some children.

"What are you doing?" she asked.

"Looking for sea shells," they said. "Beautiful ones."

Sea shells? the princess thought. "I will look with you." She soon found what fun it is to find shells, and after a great deal of looking she found a very old shell, worn by the sea and very, very lustrous.

"I have found my cup of pearl!" the princess declared, feeling very pleased with herself.

Then she saw a little boy crying because he could not find a pretty shell, and she gave him her special one. I can always find another, she thought, and felt even happier.

Again the princess set out. She walked and she wandered for a long while. Night came. The princess looked up and saw the moon shining, surrounded by a soft, glowing circle of light.

"There! There is my silver ring!" said the princess.

She ate a peanut butter and macaroni sandwich and two twists of licorice and made a bed for herself of pine needles and soft grasses. Soon she was fast asleep.

In the morning the princess breakfasted on pickles from her basket and wild berries gathered from the woods. Then she set out again.

The princess walked and wandered for a long while, and finally she came upon a meadow where some children were dancing barefoot in the grass.

"I would like to dance too," said the princess. "I wish I had some dancing shoes."

"You don't need shoes. Come dance with us!" said one of the children.

So the princess took off her royal hiking boots and felt light as air as she danced with the others.

"I am dancing, I am dancing," sang the happy princess. "Without any dancing shoes, I am dancing as I choose!" And she danced and she danced and she danced.

After that, the princess was very, very hungry so she ate the rest of her lunch. She had almost finished the chocolate-chip cookies when she heard a little bird chirp,

"To-whit, to-whoo, to-whit, to-whoo,
I am very hungry too!"

The princess broke her last cookie into bits and scattered the crumbs in the grass.

The little bird flew down beside her and ate all the crumbs. Then he hopped up right on her shoulder and sang,

"To-whit, to-whoo, to-whit, to-whoo.
Little girl, little friend, I thank you."

"I will come every day to feed you," promised the princess, for she knew she had found at last the singing bird she had been seeking.

Then she returned to the palace.

"Princess, where have you been? We were so worried about you!" said her grandmother and grandfather.

"And where are your royal hiking boots?" asked her father.

"Hush, all of you," said her mother. "See how happy our princess is. She has found what she went looking for."

"I have, indeed," said the princess, and she hugged her mother and father, her grandmother and grandfather.

"Tomorrow," said the happy princess, "let us go walking together, and I will show you how to find what I have found." And that is exactly what happened.

They found pearly sea shells and the ring around the moon. They danced in the meadow and fed the singing bird. And they found the princess's royal hiking boots, too, right where she had left them, and some fine rocks and twigs and pine cones to take home to the palace.

"The fun is in the finding," said the happy princess. "I will find other things another day."

And so she did.

ABOUT THE

AUTHOR   SUE ANN ALDERSON

Sue Ann Alderson has written over a dozen children's books, and has had her poems published by magazines in both Canada and the United States. Sue Ann also teaches a course in children's writing. She lives in Vancouver with her husband and two children. When she isn't writing she likes to care for her animals and travel with her children.

African Mother Goose Rhymes

by Virginia Kroll
Illustrated by Mohammed Danawi

Kalahari Days Hot

Kalahari days hot,
Kalahari days cold,
Baby in a kaross cape
Nine days old.
Block out the desert heat,
Keep out the desert cold,
Baby in a kaross cape
Nine days old.

To Market

To market, to market
To buy dates and plums.
Home again, home
To the beating of drums!

Bend a Wire

Bend a wire, bend a wire,
Coppersmith man.
Make me a bracelet
Fast as you can.
Swerve it and curve it
And add a nice charm,
So Mama will wear it
Each day on her arm.

Rock-a-Bye Baby

Rock-a-bye baby in Mama's shawl,
Snuggled up tightly, round as a ball.
When Mama bends,
You'll dip and you'll sway
Like leaves in a soft breeze
All through the day.

The Other Frog Prince

by Jon Scieszka
Illustrated by Lane Smith

Once upon a time there was a frog.

One day when he was sitting on his lily pad, he saw a beautiful princess sitting by the pond. He hopped in the water, swam over to her, and poked his head out of the weeds.

"Pardon me, O beautiful princess," he said in his most sad and pathetic voice. "I wonder if you could help me."

The princess was about to jump up and run, but she felt sorry for the frog with the sad and pathetic voice.

So she asked, "What can I do to help you, little frog?"

"Well," said the frog. "I'm not really a frog, but a handsome prince who was turned into a frog by a spell. And the spell can only be broken by the kiss of a beautiful princess."

persuasoria

stellifera

fly

The princess thought about this for a second, then lifted the frog from the pond and kissed him.

"I was just kidding," said the frog. He jumped back into the pond and the princess wiped the frog slime off her lips. The End.

ABOUT THE AUTHOR

JON SCIESZKA

Jon Scieszka had many jobs before he became a full-time writer, including being a house painter and teacher. Jon says, "Someday I might write for adults, but I think kids are the greatest audience for a writer. No one can believe a story or love one as much as a kid does."

New Tales from Old:
Amazing Animation

by Gary Hurst, as told to Catherine Rondina
Illustrated by Renée Mansfield

Animated films, or cartoons, are a new kind of storytelling. The people who draw cartoons are called animators. That's because their drawings "animate" characters—bring them to life on the screen.

How do they do it? Film director Gary Hurst has animated many cartoons, including **Care Bears, Babar, Rupert the Bear,** and **Franklin.** Here's what he says about creating animated stories.

2. The Storyboard

When the script is ready, a director like me is put in charge of the project. First, I approve the script. Then I take it to the story department. There the storyboard artist and I do rough drawings called *blueprints*. They show how each character is going to look. For example, we would decide how long Red Riding Hood's hair will be or how scary the wolf's face should look. We display the drawings on a large wall board called a *storyboard*.

1. The Story and the Script

Every good film begins with a good story idea. Let's say we decided to turn the fairy tale "Little Red Riding Hood" into an animated film. A group of writers called *scriptwriters* would turn the story into a script. A script is like a play. It has all the *dialogue*, or lines, the actors need to read.

3. The Sound

I then help hire the actors who give the characters their voices. The actors read the script aloud together, and their voices are recorded onto a tape. Meanwhile, a *sound technician* chooses sound effects, and a music composer creates the music for the cartoon. A technician then records the voices, sound effects, and music onto one tape, called the *soundtrack*.

4. Layout and Background

Next, the *layout artists* do the drawings that show where each character will be placed in a scene. For example, they would draw where Red Riding Hood and the Wolf are to be placed when they meet for the first time in the woods.

The layout drawings are sent to the *background artists*. Their job is to draw the background scenes such as the forest and the Grandmother's cottage.

5. Animation

Now the animators make the characters move. They create many, many drawings of each character's actions. The finished sets of drawings are filmed on video tape and checked to make sure the movement is clear.

6. Painting

After that, the *ink and paint artists* paint the cartoon. They decide all sorts of things about color—for example, how red Little Red Riding Hood's cape will be. The artists "paint" on computer. A machine called a scanner inputs the drawings into the computer. Then the artists "paint" the drawings by clicking a mouse. All the colors are in the computer's memory.

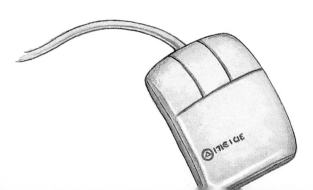

7. Filming and Copying

After the drawings are painted, they are filmed onto video tape. This video goes to the editing department, and all the sounds, special effects, music, and pictures are matched together onto one tape. The tape is sent out to be copied, then it goes to television stations for broadcasting.

It would take us over six months to make Little Red Riding Hood into a half-hour cartoon. We would have to make between 14 000 and 25 000 drawings. It sounds like a lot of hard work, and it is. But it's great to see a cartoon you brought to life right there on the television screen!

The Three Little Pigs

Once there were three little pig sisters named Mary, Emily, and Ray. Emily helped Mary make a house out of books and they lived there together. Ray made a house too.

One day, the Big Bad Wolf knocked on Mary and Emily's front door. He said, "Let me in."

They answered, "No!"

"Then I will huff and puff and blow your house down."

Mary and Emily were scared so they ran out of their back door into Ray's house. The wolf followed them and tried to blow down Ray's house. When he could not blow the house down he climbed up on the roof. There he tripped and fell down the chimney into a pot of hot water. This gave him such a big surprise that he jumped up and ran out of the door. He never bothered the pigs again.

Adda Huang
Grade 3

I like writing because it's great. I learn new words, and I learn how to spell them and remember them.

Adda Huang

Dear Three Bears

Dear Three Bears,

Hi! I am sorry for eating your porridge and for breaking your chair. I am also sorry for sleeping in baby bear's bed. If you ever invite me over I will not do any damage. Next Saturday my family and I are going berry picking. If you want to come with me you can. Maybe my family can come over today and my dad can make you new chairs and I can make your beds. My mom can make some porridge for you. Oh, well, I have to go now to baby-sit. I guess I have to say bye now. Bye.

Sincerely,
Goldilocks

Kelly Pratt
Grade 3

In school this year, we wrote a story from the point of view of the person who made the problems. I did "Goldilocks and the Three Bears." I love to do things about fairy tales, especially "Goldilocks and the Three Bears."

Kelly Pratt